Call Me When You Get Home

Dazhona Hodge

BookLeaf Publishing

India | USA | UK

Presentation by *BookLeaf Publishing*

Web: www.bookleafpub.com

E-mail: info@bookleafpub.com

ISBN: 9789360944247

First edition 2024

To Asiah, Khloe, and Demonte....

Don't Forget to call me when you get home.

and lastly To my mother...I'll always be here to take you home.

ACKNOWLEDGEMENT

I couldn't have brought this poetry collection to life without the love and support of some incredible people.

First and foremost, I want to express my deepest gratitude to my Grandma Shirley and my Auntie Kyessa for always believing in me and encouraging my creative endeavors. Your unwavering support has been my rock throughout this journey.

To my Best Friend Cam and my favorite Cousin Jealisa, thank you for being my sounding board, my cheerleaders, and my inspiration. Your words of encouragement and honest feedback in my life have shaped this collection in ways I can't even begin to express.

A special shoutout goes to my Nanny, whose guidance and wisdom have been invaluable. Your belief in my talent and your gentle nudges in the right direction have made all the difference.

I also want to extend my heartfelt appreciation to the amazing team at BookLeaf Publishing. Thank you for giving me the opportunity and helping me bring this dream to fruition.

To my Dad, Thank You for everything. I am so grateful to have you in my life. Words can't express the amount of gratitude that I have for you always being there for me. …. just thank you.

Last but not least, to you, dear reader, thank you for picking up this book and giving my words a chance to resonate with you. Your support means the world to me, and I hope that these poems touch your heart in a profound way.

With love and gratitude,

Dazhona

PREFACE

Hey boo! Before you dive into the enchanting world of "Call Me When You Get Home," I wanted to share a few words with you.

This collection of poems is like a window into my heart and soul, where emotions run wild and words dance on the page. Each poem is a piece of me, crafted with love and vulnerability. So, I'm sensitive about my shit. I've poured my deepest thoughts and experiences into these verses, hoping to connect with your own journey and stir something within you. Whether you find solace, inspiration, or simply a moment of reflection, my greatest wish is that these words touch your heart in a meaningful way. If you don't take away anything, well .....That's on you. Read it again.

So, grab a cozy spot, open these pages, and let the magic of poetry unfold. Thank you for joining me on this adventure!

...or don't. IDGAF.

The Calling of The Muses

Heavenly Father,

Sing to me, O Holy Spirit, of the woman of
twists and turns,
The hero who wandered far and wide, after the
fall of Herself.
Tell me, Holy Spirit, of her trials and
tribulations,
Of the battles fought and the gods she
encountered.
Grant me your divine voice, O Holy Spirit, so
that I may recount
The story of she, the cunning and resourceful,

And the journey that led her back to her
homeland.

in your name I pray.

Amen

Reciprocate

I would go to the end of the world with you, but
you won't do the same.
I'd give you anything to the point where I feel
lame.
I'd always come for you because I love you.
I'd never put anybody above you.
but I can't fight the feeling that that feeling is
one-sided.
I'm afraid to tell you things because I'm not the
one that you confide in.

I don't understand how you can't relate. all I
ever wanted was you to just reciprocate.

The Damned Man

I love you. I really do! From your head to your toes. you're really my boo. I have no problem doing for you, but at the rate we're going we can't live in truth.

I care about you and I'd love to be with you. But
spirit won't allow it to ensue. a new soul
contract? that'll never do because god and
heaven wouldn't approve.

you treat her like garbage yet so sweet to me.
That's the only red flag that I need, but honey

You're like hot sauce on the tongue everything
about you is just so much fun. and baby you
make me feel like a natural womannnnnnn.

but this is cursed and it'll never move. It's only
going to get worse as time continues.
I hope in another realm I get to see you. I hope
you remember me in the next life. I hope my
soul is familiar to you in its own right.

I hope you're my friend and you understand and
still play the cards that were dealt to your hand.
You are a wonderful man. I just really hope you
understand.

Love johnny….your very good friend.

Wanderlust

I find solace in the journey when I'm wandering.
Just walking endlessly. stumbling upon whatever
the day has to gift me. I can be here. I can be
there. My mind is always everywhere.
but I'll just keep walking. Waiting for something
to happen. waiting to come across another world
to tap in.
My spirit is lost but my soul is around. Just
walking. Just waiting. Hoping to be found.

don't know why I'm here quite frankly. I just
know there are some places I can't be.
The journey seems long, but I can be wrong.
so… I'll just wait.

Affirmations Of a Baddie

I've been that bitch and always will be
money & abundance is always attracted to me
I was created to live in luxury
All the girlies look up to me.
I'm that bitch and a half
leaving everyone gagged
My Career is thriving
my energy is vibing
I look amazing and so does my money

Chord Cutting

I cut this cord already! yet you still in my damn
space. you should've picked me in the first damn
place.
You're a waste of my time and a waste of space.
you want me to fwu but you play in my face.

Fuck youuuuu ain't never did nothing for me anyway and now your goofy ass has a baby on the way? and you expect me to still fwy the same?
Every time I leave it's in a frown but I still slide cuz imma damn clown and I do like having you around but my loneliness is what keeps this bound.
but nah I can't fwy at some point I have to start being true…to my self take care of my wealth and my health. Play the card I was dealt.
I hope I never see you again you could never be there for me. I wish you the best but please spare me. I owe myself that cuz you truly suck. I'd rather just put myself out there…and try my luck

Let's Go Out!

You bring the sun and I bring the fun!
I gotta lil weed what else you need?
We can slide here or there
I got some gas we can go anywhere!
We can get a bottle and live foreva
but I'm down for whatevas clever
we can talk and confide
but it's niggas outside!!!!
We can go out to eat
you had the last one this one's my treat
Let's go be in the mix
your company is everything I wouldn't miss
we can eat until we get gout
I'm just happy we went out

Home Alone

In the depths of solitude, I find my retreat,
A silent companion, my heart's steady beat.
Whispers of longing, echoes in the night,
Loneliness embraces me, a bittersweet plight.

In solitude's embrace, I search for solace,
A dance with my thoughts, a quiet space.
Yet amidst the silence, a longing persists,
For connection and warmth, to cease the mist.

Loneliness, a reminder of our human need,
To be seen, understood, and gently freed.
But fear not, dear friend, for you're not alone,
In this vast world, hearts await to be known.

Reach out, embrace the bonds that await,
Kindred spirits, to share your fate.
For in the depths of loneliness, hope can reside,
A reminder that connection will soon coincide.

Remember, honey, you're never truly alone,
In this journey of life, hearts will find their own.
Hold on to hope, let it guide your way,
And loneliness will fade, like the break of day.
you're never truly alone, for God is guiding you
all the way home.

bye. get tf on.

Manipulation is only cool when I do it. I got good intentions.

Friend of Yours

We're friends and I relate to you so much
The time we spend together ....the way we
always keep in touch.
We're friends and yes you can have whatever I
have
Everything is worth it after a good laugh

We're friends Yet it seems pretty shady on your
side
The subtle joke here and there that makes my
eyes go to the side

We're friends yet something's off right now
Idk if we're meant to be and Idk if it's loud

We're friends but I have to learn to set
boundaries
I need to take time to myself your subscription is
high and I can't afford the fees
We're friends but I think we have to grow
Separation may be good for us right now. We
might have to go.

I haven't always had the best friends and I
wasn't always the best either
I hope you're doing good all the way to the end
and Even if we never be cool again, you were
still my friend. It might not have been to the end
but I hope that we set the tone to begin again.

Soul Cry

Got so much pain, where to start?
I'm tryna find the light but everyday it gets Dark
They give me pain in exchange for the remains
of my heart
Every time the good comes it's bad right behind
it
So scared to be elated cause somebody's there to
snatch it
I'm broken in pieces and I can't explain it I pray
to the lord that he forgives me for living so
shameless.

Staying up and thinking in the middle of the
night
How can I pick up all these pieces that's my life
I wanna say fuck it but then again I gotta try
I try I tryyyyyyyyyyyy

The Gardener

I was a seed that didn't grow fast enough for
you.
Your impatience didn't let you see my
petals...Are they pretty yet?

The Poorest Man I Couldn't Afford

See now...
I'm a Capricorn, so I tend to look at relationships
as transactions.
I give to you, you give to me
We should both be in states of satisfaction.
Me, personally, I like to trick off in energy
My love is always complimentary and I be on
my lil boo ever so tenderly
but with you... I noticed that is something that I
will never see.
Some people are so poor all they have is money.
And I've been where you are when my skies
weren't so sunny, and quite frankly wasn't shit
funny.

But what about me? Giving you my energy is
like paying my fees. And you can't even be nice
to me?
I gave and I gave my account in the negative and
I must be replenished. Now I'm down and out
with nothing and you're seemingly unblemished.
No phone calls, Dates, or even a listening ear?
Nothing's worse than realizing you spent your
last with matilda's dad
because lemons is all they had
Now look at me...going out sad and really down
bad.

OMFG

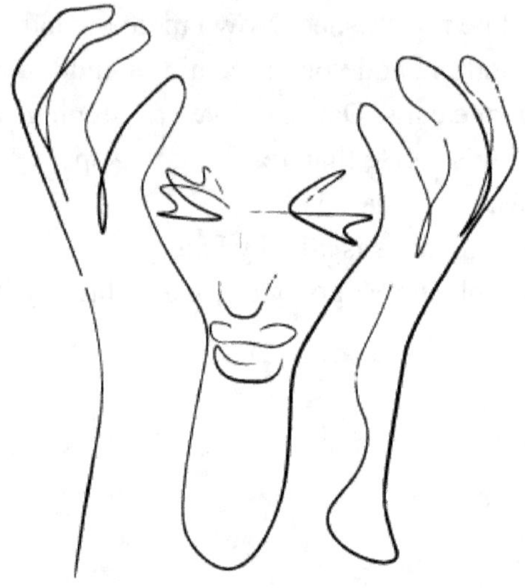

I just wanna be left alone. please for the love of
god leave me alone.

A Single Bedside Table

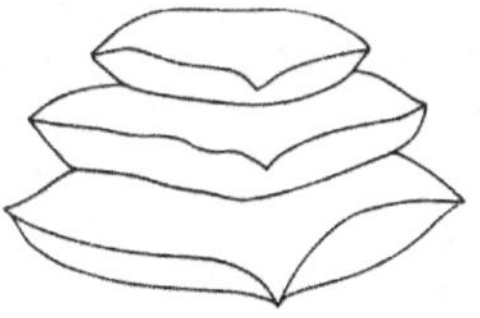

You are so damn cute!
I've got to bring you home....
Now I don't just be sold on things like this but
you got me Tight
you mean I can borrow you for one night?
No contract?
Will the owners be upset?
There's no contact?
well...I enjoyed you lots, but the time has come.
You must go back. I'm one and done.

I missed you

The smell the storm left behind lingers as we embrace each other... The unimaginable awaits us once we're truly done.

I'm just a Girl

Idk what's going on.
Time waits for none, when will this become fun?

Alternate Realities

I believe I know you from somewhere.
We've done this before.
In another reality, this worked out
Your presence can warm a chicago night.
The words you speak are as sweet as honey and
might.

you're so familiar.
In every essence of every timeline you were
mine
In a lot of universes we were fine
In a sense we're immortal.
we've gone through portals and hinted at
schrödinger
because we've done this already.
In many lifetimes we've loved each other.
How do I know?
The Cosmos told me so....

A trip to The Big Time Capsule

They paused my time.... but the world kept going. They didn't wait for me.

Run

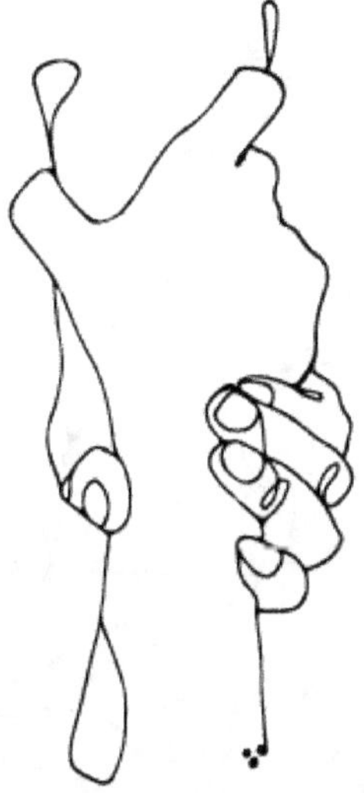

Let's run from ourselves! We can make a run
from our ego and pride. Will you come?

Fight Night

I'm tired of yo ass
so let's just lay it all out just not too fast
You're a thorn in my side and at this point I'm
thinking of new places to reside
You've been on my nerves for a few months
now
we were good as a couple no but you knew three
was a crowd
I'm supposed to forgive you cuz it's my fault?
Yet this behavior won't come to a halt
You do what you want and fuck how I feel right?
It's ok for me to go to bed sad every night?

Sobriety Society

How can I be a woman of virtue with all these
vices?
How did I even get all these vices?
When I look back, I remember the first day I met
y'all but when did y'all become the loves of my
life?
Was I looking for you? When did things get out
of hand?
This was never part of the plan
but on the other hand

am I going to do what I do best and lie to myself
cuz you know I can stop whenever…imma
uh…just start next week.
or am I too weak and meek to overcome this
peak
cuz I just need a lil bit to get to where I need to
be
But I just need to get to tomorrow

My only destination is tomorrow
…just let me get to tomorrow
please.

Johnny's 3am prayer

Heavenly Father,

I come to you as your humble servant. I ask that you fill my heart with joy because I've forgotten to smile this week. Do the same for my family and friends.

I ask that you fill me with discernment and wisdom to make better decisions for myself because

We know what I've done in the past.

I ask that you remove any body that is against me and not for the prosperity of my life.

O' God you are the alpha and the omega and
deserve my praise everyday. You are the beacon
of light I forget I have everyday.
O' God please protect me and cover me in your
blood.
O' God I've been so ungrateful and you have
blessed me every step of the way.
O' God I love you. You have never taken your
hands off me even when I didn't deserve it.
O' God you have showed me nothing but the
sweetest grace
O' God you have made sure my heart stayed the
way that it was.
You are the love that I receive and give
everyday. My life is bountiful and beautiful and
I have
nobody to thank but you. I may not have a lot of
money, but you've always helped me find a way.
You have never left or forsaken me. Everything I
touch is golden. All praise be to the most high!
in Jesus name I pray….

in my head

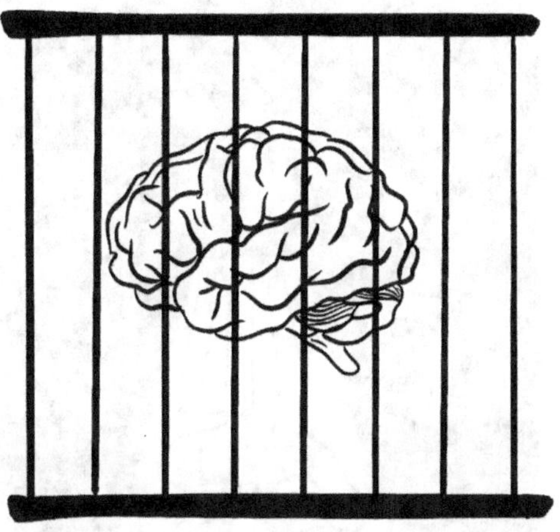

The horrors of this place consume me. I keep
running around in circles and replaying
everything.

It's like I'm forever out of bounds but this thing
is attached to me. I hear everything that I fear all
at once. Something is always lurking in the
shadows in here but I'm trapped. I can't get out.
If I tell anybody then I for sure will never get out
of here. It's seeping into my reality and they'll
discover who I really am eventually.
FUCK
They can't discover who I really am….
They just can't….

SHADE

My tongue can cut like razor blades, but her
tongue is like venom.
A physical war zone where subliminal are
thrown, so childish yet so grown.
Remarks so slick you gotta do a double-take. "Is
this bitch coming for me? is she tryna bake?"
She says she's just joking but it's giving hate.

Now my whole body is stinging because she tryna treat me. I can't go out like that. I can't let her defeat me.

"who the fuck does she think she is? don't she know I got her dirt?" Now I gotta load my glock and hit her where it hurts?

Now, Imma laugh it off and say "I'm just playin'", but sweetie don't come for me is all I'm saying.

You say what you want because you've got the gall. But you'll see how people really feel and that's the shade of it all.

KARMA SOS

Karma, I know you seen that so what you gon do? It's been a few months and they've gotten everything new!
You just gon let them get away with all that they did to me? It's like you helped them out…right

back on to their feet.
What about me? I'm the victim. Do I need to
call the police and put them in the system?
Nah I ain't gon do that…imma leave it alone,
but let them come back and call my phone.
Imma do them so dirty…Imma do them so
wrong. And it's all your fault karma…because
you
took too long.

Poor Af

If it ain't one thing, it's another. I might have to
borrow $3 from my lil brother.
I don't make enough anywhere at all. Shit….I
gotta rob peter to pay paul. I'm working 16-hr
days…there's so much I have to pay.
This shit sucks! When's it going to be my turn?
Have I not been good? Has it not been earned?
Stood in the mirror and tried to manifest twice,
but the shit not working so just put my whole
life
in rice.
I know I know…Trust the process right? I could
really bust this move and be good by tonight.
Nah imma just be cool and wait on a dime. I just
really hope soon is my time.

You made me do it

Didn't wanna leave
but you pushed me that far
Now it's all my fault?

Weak

Everyone talks about love, but no one speaks on
that downside
That one emotion that sends you on a ride like a
landslide. It's called pride.
The pride that you set aside to give them the
impression that you can abide by any means to
keep them by your side.
Or when you feel the need to beg and plead and
say things like "I know I tend to live
lackadaisically…but if you can just stay with
me…"
But they don't fulfill those needs and now
they're self-proclaimed as free and you die in
multiples of 3 and all you can say is "well I'll be
here if you need me"
Pathetic right? All that shit hurt right? When you
threw that line out and they didn't bite? When
you showed up to the frontline and they didn't
fight? When your days were dark and you

couldn't bum a light? or when their new boo's
got the nerve to be so damn polite?
Now you must question everything you know
about love … "was it heaven sent from up
above?
Did it really clear my skin or was it just my
dove? Did they even care from jump to ever be a
fit
for me like a glove?"
It's honestly pure insanity because your future
sun will just be vanity. because now you're
trying
to find a man to be everything you wanted in
him.

Hot Mess Express

Glitter glitter glitter from the eyebrows down.
makeup caked on to make a dead woman frown.
sitting in this mirror, did I tell you I was
drinking brown?

If I keep spraying this versace, you just might drown.

everybody's been hittin my line. y'all calling to tell me that I'm fine as wine? The lace front couldn't be felt. I look cleaner than the board of health.

Baby girl, you stalk my snap …you peak and you lurk. so did you see me hop out the car? Did you see me twerk?

Lyin, cussin, drinkin, and smokin is what I do everyday. My lashes are so long if I blink I just might fly away.

Lips smothered in gloss..If he leaves, baby that ain't no loss.

Nails longer than a 10-mile race. Oh you got something to say? wanna get hit in your face?

I've got bundles in every texture. It wouldn't be me if I wasn't hella extra.

You can say what you want about me I can care less but once you get to know me…all aboard the hot mess express.

...And just like that

a way was just made. Another reason to be
grateful because
I did the work and you met me half way
you through it up in the air and I dunked it.
we're like shaq and kobe or sum
you blessed me immensely as if it were nothing.
how did that even happen? what were the odds?

I owe everything to you O' God.
you led me here
I have nothing to fear. walking with you has
been a blast my dear.

if love ever decides to visit me again….

I sure hope they stay. even on days when I've been getting in my own way. These days I can't afford to play but I'd wish you'd stop by just to say hey.

Long Walk Home

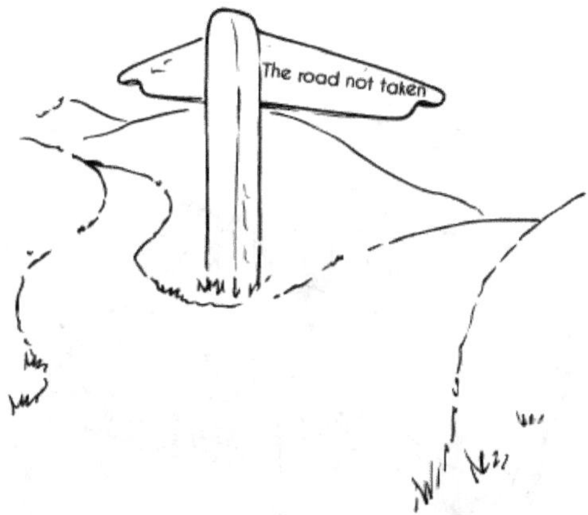

Do you have your keys? Do you have your
purse? Girl you look like you're fresh out of a
hearse.
The sun is shining so bright it's like it's taking
aim. I know you're hungover, but you need to
take
this walk of shame. your phone is dead, but
would it even ring? Now you know damn well
you
were just a fling.
Gone ahead and have a seat on this train and
ain't no need to feeling any pain because owning
your shit is a skill you'll learn to hone, but until
then child it's gonna be a long walk home.

Apologies to Me

I'm all over the place somehow I'm everywhere
all at once but here.
I hear you talking but I can't find my ear. I
seemed to have lost my eyes they were attached
to my tears.
my legs and arms have gone on their own.
Mindlessly moving while leaving my head on its
own.
While knowing that my heart does not trust me
and just wants to be left alone.
I get it.
I've done them wrong because I wasn't strong
and I just had to go along.

And as for them…they didn't either. They didn't
worship you, they were just "eager".
My ignorance isn't bliss, yet I really didn't
know. I've been poisoning you since I was 3
years old.
BUT
I'm here to apologize to my thighs because if I
keep eating these fries they'll meet their
inevitable demise.
I've never been great with goodbyes you can ask
those other guys.
To my hands, you've always complied.
and to my yoni below me you've always been
the homie. you've never left me lonely.
and to my face, darling you've never missed. but
I can't help but reminisce on what I once was
before this.
As I watch my soul chip away bit by bit, it
begins its journey off into the abyss.

Time Out

Time waits for no one. As I barely hang on to shore, it's like I'm getting older but I'm not having
fun anymore. Don't have the same attitude as I once had before, and even though I'm in my prime I'm still running out of time because I've yet to call something worthwhile mine.

New Shoes

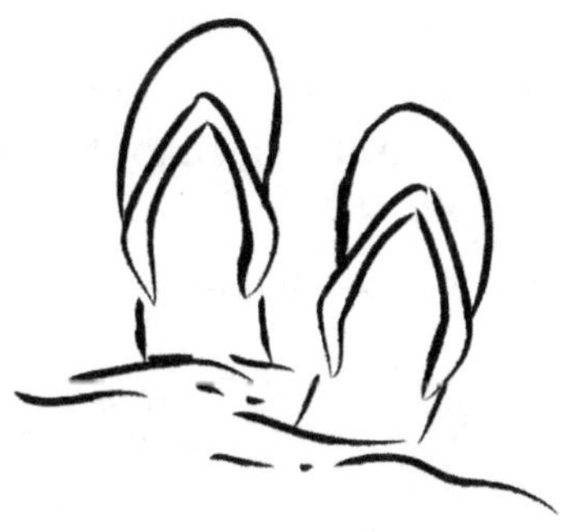

"hey, I haven't heard from you. what's going on?
what's new? nothing much with me but I got
some new shoes. it's been one of those weeks ya
know? when I'm under the weather; when I'm
feeling blue.
I would say that I miss you, but I'd rather talk
about my shoes. Did I tell you they were jimmy
choo? Can I ask if you think about me and you?
but I mean shiddd I don't care I know you got a
lot going on and the last time we talked the vibe
was all wrong.

but anyways what do you think? Do my shoes
look nice? Do you like this color? Will these do?
will they suffice?
I seen the shoes your girl posted yesterday they
were aiight
Did you buy them for her? Can you come over?
Do you want to spend the night?
I mean I don't care if you don't I Know how
things can be. I…just wanted to show you my
shoes
but g …don't forget about me?"

Queen of LSD

Good vibes looming in with amber lights from
the eway.
No backroads just back woods on a night soaked
in dussé.
Arizona cans filled with guts and ashes seem to
work.
We're holding hands whilst biting down percs.

somehow trying to ignore pain that hurts.
He moves on down to hold my knee, but shit I
can't comprehend my veins are still holding
ecstasy.
His foot on the gas…he's doing the dash with
the air on blast.
Trap music knockin as my head begins a noddin
Don't know where we goin. Man I hope he
doesn't think I'm going.
In this environment I seem to thrive. I think I'm
the queen of lake shore drive.

Proverbz

Now Class What did we learn?
That we can be smart with what we earn.
Take that check, put 20% in savings, 30% on
wants and 50% on needs.
Don't be afraid, babygirl, to sew those seeds.
Never let a man tell you he doesn't want you
twice.
You can demand what you want. its not about
being nice.
When you work hard everyday your bell will be
the next rung.
Always have your own money anything he gives
you is extra.
You don't need validation just yours and your
own.
Own all of your bullshit because it's yours and
yours alone.
Don't let anybody ruffle your feathers
Keeping your composure and your grace is what
he measures.
Take a loss like a boss and don't dwell on the
"L"
If you never take that step forward, you've
already begun to fail.

Don't get discouraged of people's opinion of
you.
You know who you are and you know what you
do.
Date the one that loves you and not the one you
love.
9 times out of 10 that's the one from up above.
Don't ever look down on anyone because those
tables will turn.
Who are you to judge when you're still trying to
learn?
You don't have to prove your worth. You don't
have to struggle for love.
Don't Die for that respect or really the lack
thereof.
Don't feel bad for using your rainy day fund.
That was the whole point of you having it.
It could be worse. you could have none.
If he's stuck between you and someone else. Let
him pick them.
You're always the first choice just not to him.
When y'all arguing, and it's hurting a little too
much?
Those girls aren't your friends they've been
waiting for this stuff.
When people want to leave, let them go.

They may not be aligned with where you're
about to go.

Do what you love but work is not life.
Don't go to an early grave if it is not your time.
Don't let nobody play in your face.
You may not have it all right now, but it isn't a
race.
Social media is fake. Don't let it make you think
that your blessings aren't on the way.
Call your mom or Call your dad.
It's not always about you. They might be sad.
Don't max out that credit card you'll regret it
immensely.
Only use it in times of emergencies.
If he shows you love, reciprocate it.
If not leave him alone and let someone else
appreciate it.
Put yourself first. You have to live this life.
Don't be tryna race to be just anybody's wife.
If accountability is something you lack, don't
justify your actions with feelings for they are not
fact.
Don't know where to start or where to go?
Be who you needed when you were 9 years old.
Don't beg for a call. Don't beg for a text.
He wouldn't let you do that if he wasn't on to
the next.
Be in the present. Be in the now.
Nothing's ever worth staying with a frown.
If they're acting funny, take them at their word.

People always show their hands no matter what
occurred.
On the outside you're beautiful but on the inside
so rotten.
How you treat others is telling and is usually not
forgotten.
Do that shadow work and work on your inner
self the most.
So when they see you again they'll think they've
seen a ghost. Who you are on the inside
matters the most.
When you get the blessing no need to boast. Just
thank god sincerely with a single toast.

I know you really like him, I know that's your
boo, but you're still not his girl because he's just
not
that into you.
Don't go changing everything thinking he will
notice.
You're going to hate yourself and that's not even
the motive.
Pay your bills on time if you got it.
Don't let them pile up. Don't get behind sis.
Don't fight fire with fire protect your peace.
Remove yourself from them with anger because
that's not something you should keep.
You don't get anything from being rude. Don't
be too proud to check yourself and your attitude.

I'm sorry they hurt you and the things they did,
but it's your responsibility to start your healing
process.
If you're having acne all over your face, try
drinking water and change that pillowcase.
Start that business you won't regret it. You can
have all you need once you build that business
credit.
I tell you these things because I was too
hardheaded to listen and learn.
Now take these gems and pass them on like
proverbs.

Call Me When You Get Home

And when you find it, so pure and true,
When happiness embraces you, like a sky so
blue,
Remember these words, a message from afar,
"Call me when you get home," like a guiding
star.

For if someone discovers the secret you seek,
The true essence of happiness, so gentle and
meek,
Let them reach out, let them share the delight,
So you too can bask in its radiant light.

Keep searching, with hope in your heart,
For true happiness awaits, ready to impart,
Its magic and wonder, its warmth and its glow,
In the simplest of moments, let your happiness
grow.

I hope I get to experience this happiness
wherever I roam, but if I don't and you do

Call me when you get home.

* 9 7 8 9 3 6 0 9 4 4 2 4 7 *